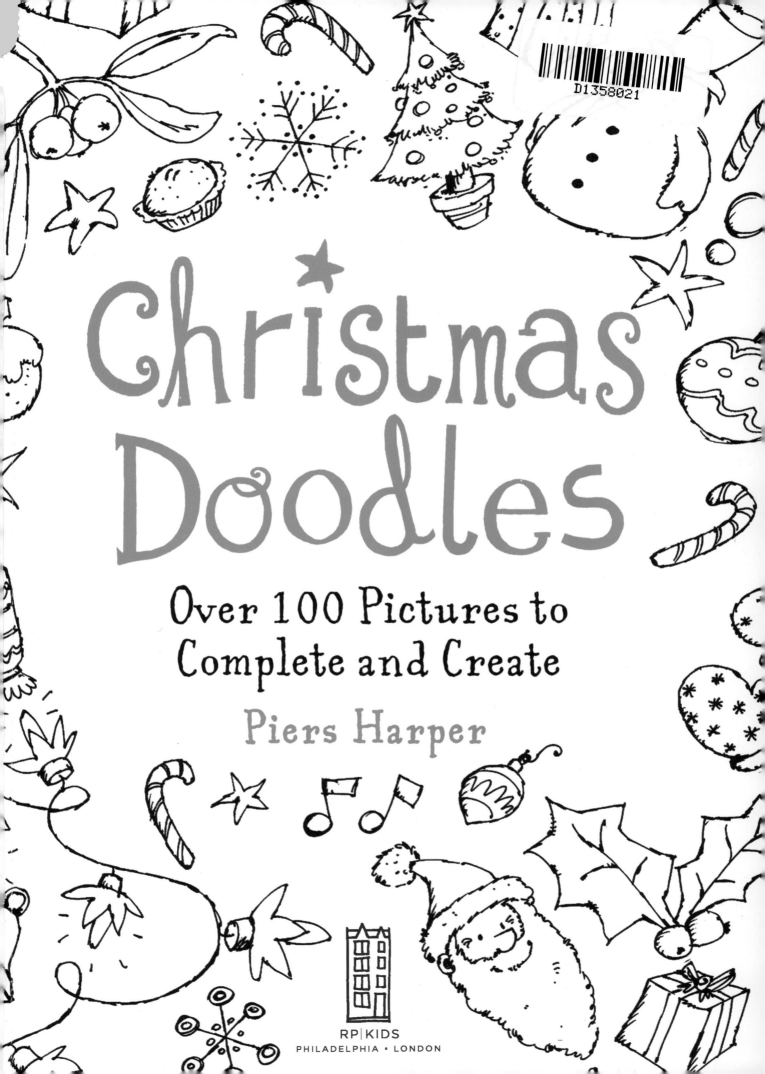

Christmas Doodles

Over 100 Pictures to Complete and Create

Piers Harper

RP | KIDS
PHILADELPHIA • LONDON

This book was first published in Great Britain by Buster Books,
an imprint of Michael O'Mara Books Limited, 9 Lion Yard, Tremadoc Road, London SW4 7NQ, 2008.

First published in the United States by Running Press Book Publishers, 2008.

Printed in China

Books published by Running Press are available at special discounts for bulk purchases in the United States
by corporations, institutions, and other organizations. For more information, please contact
the Special Markets Department at the Perseus Books Group, 2300 Chestnut Street, Suite 200,
Philadelphia, PA 19103, or call (800) 810-4145, ext. 5000, or e-mail special.markets@perseusbooks.com.

ISBN 978-0-7624-5656-7

Illustrated by Piers Harper

9 8 7 6 5 4 3 2 1
Digit on the right indicates the number of this printing

This edition published by:
Running Press Kids
An Imprint of Running Press Book Publishers
A Member of the Perseus Books Group
2300 Chestnut Street
Philadelphia, PA 19103–4371

Visit us on the web!
www.runningpress.com/kids

What is on top of the tree?

It's time to build some snowmen.

Heap the bowl with sweets.

What is in the toy-shop window?

Who is coming for Christmas?

Put on a pantomime.

Give us party hats.

Decorate your Advent calendar.

What is inside the doors?

Draw Santa a bushy beard.

Decorate the cookies.

Ornaments or puddings?

Fill the sky with snow.

What are the elves making?

Hide presents in the house.

Cover the gifts in pretty paper.

Fill the sky with stars . . .

. . . and add chimneys for Santa.

What is for Christmas breakfast?

Design a Christmas e-greeting.

Who is Mom kissing under the mistletoe?

Yikes—what a Christmas sweater!

Decorate the stockings.

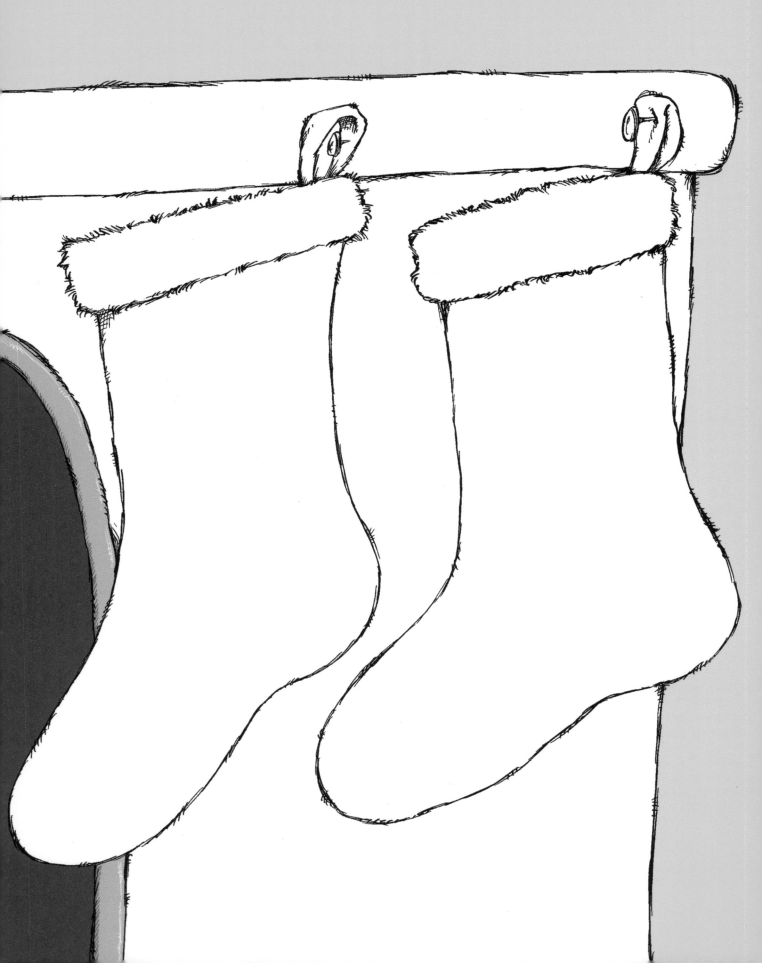

What is in the snow globe?

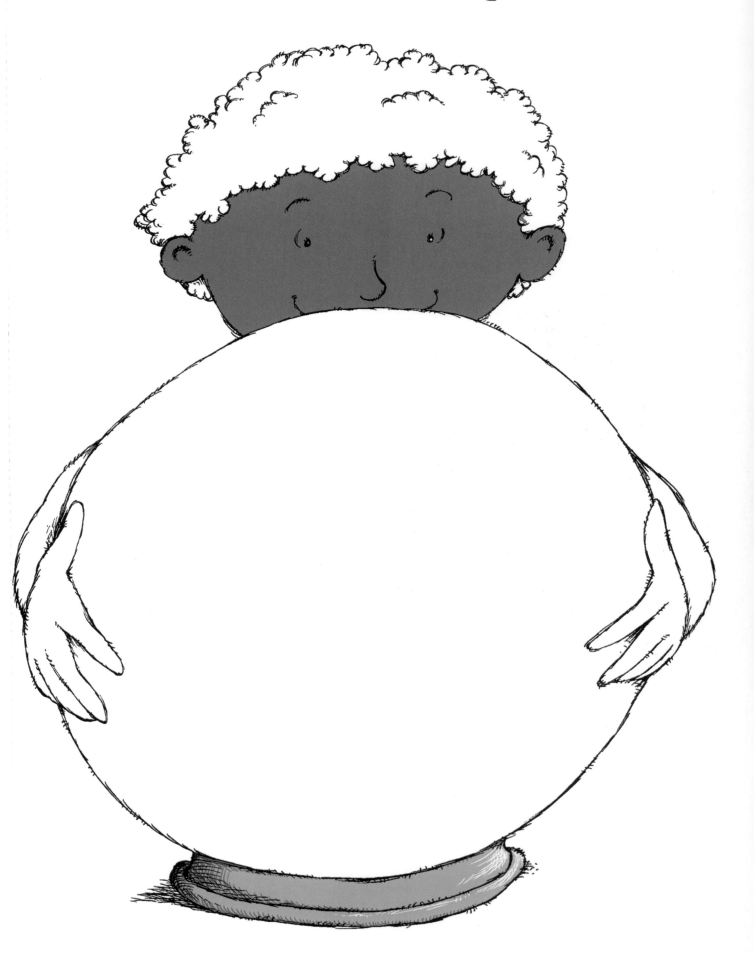

Who threw that snowball?

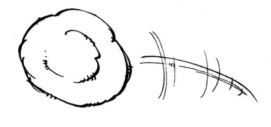

Build the world's best snowman.

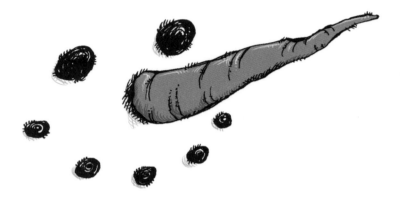

Decorate the ornaments.

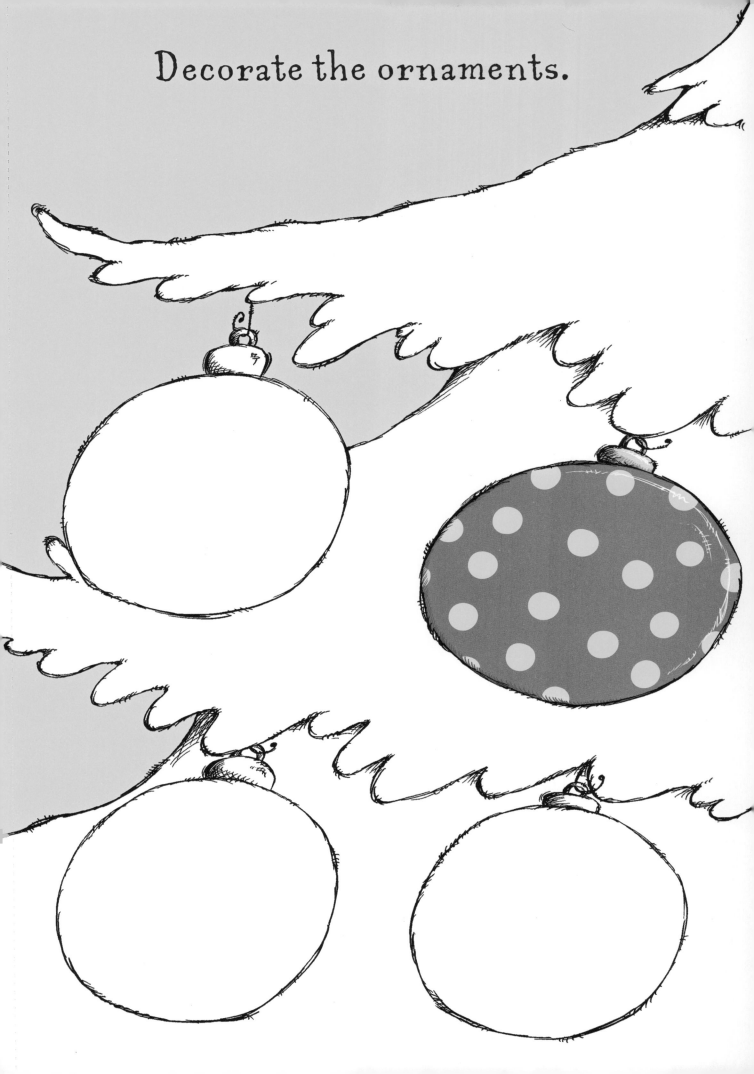

Do they like their presents?

What was left out for Santa?

Can you complete Santa?

Who slipped on the ice?

Design your own seasonal stamps.

What Christmas movie did you watch?

Give the reindeer some antlers.

Decorate the windows.

Jump out of bed on
Christmas morning!

Decorate the tree.

What treats are in the cupboard?

Decorate the Christmas cake.

Design your own Christmas card.

Fill the plate with holiday treats.

Stack up the snowballs.

Pile up the packages.

Draw the tallest tree in the forest.

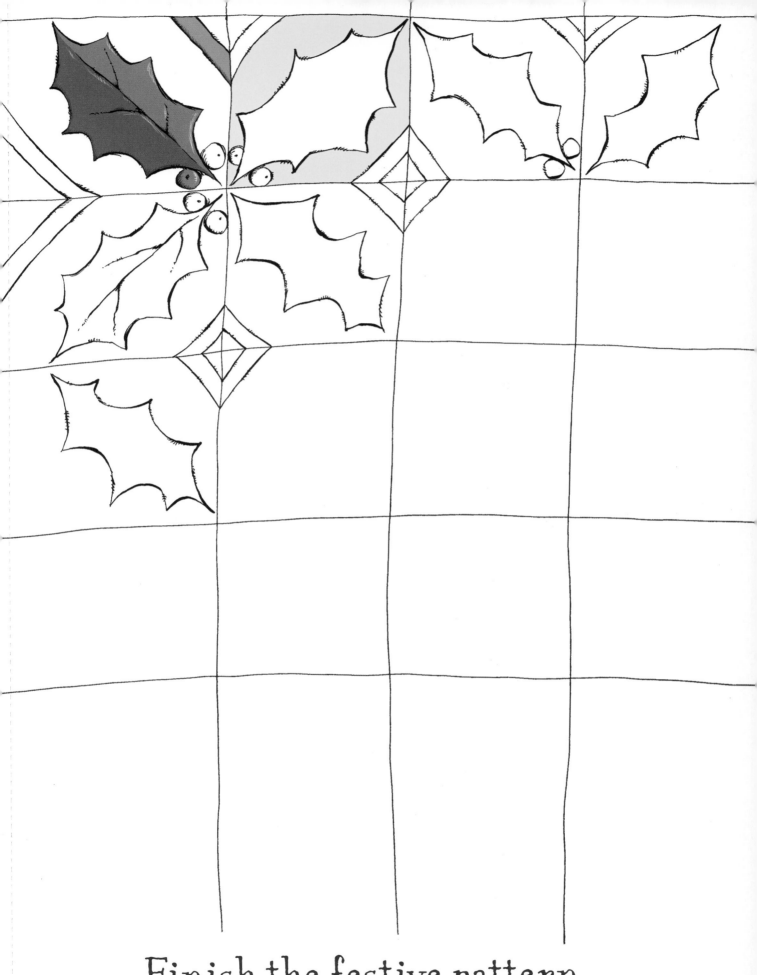

Finish the festive pattern.

Fancy dress!

Whose footprints?

What presents did the pets get?

Ding-dong bells.

What games are they playing?

Decorate the bedroom.

Make the fireplace festive.

Cover the house with fairy lights.

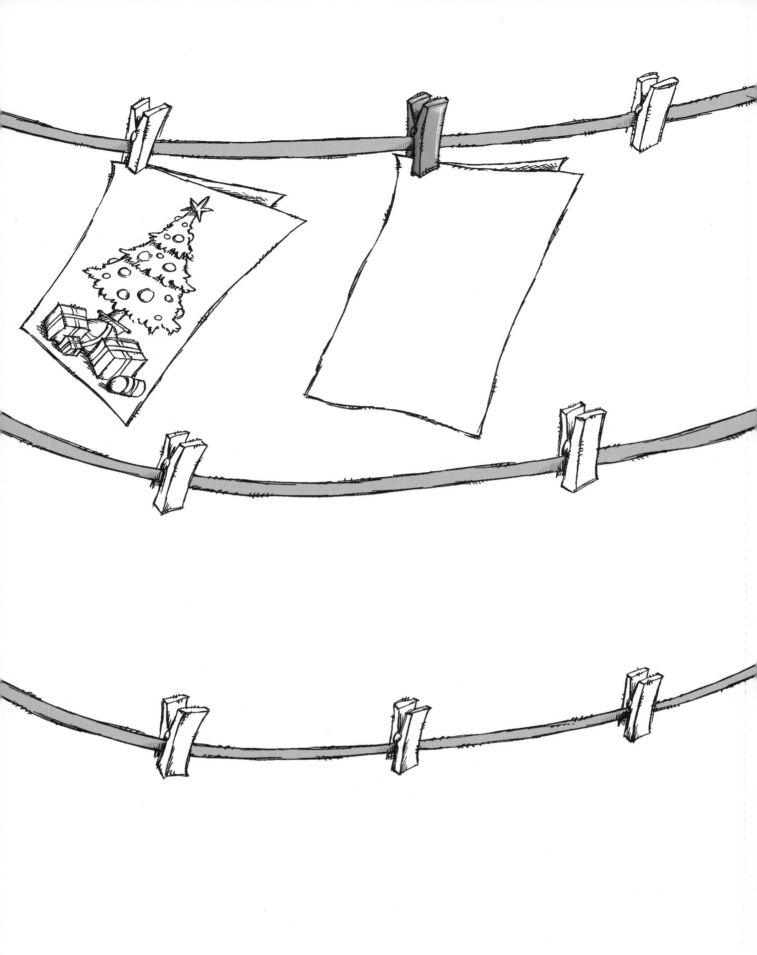

Draw the cards on the line.

Finish the wreath on the door.

Design your own wrapping paper.

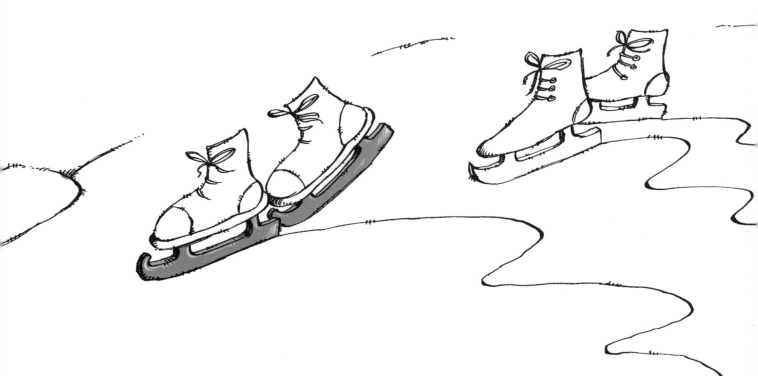

Give them great skating outfits.

Write a Christmas poem.

What an amazing ice sculpture!

Look at Dad's Christmas socks!

Pile the presents under the tree.

Draw your favorite Christmas gifts.

Can you finish Rudolph?

Color in the candy canes.

Add more Christmas lights.

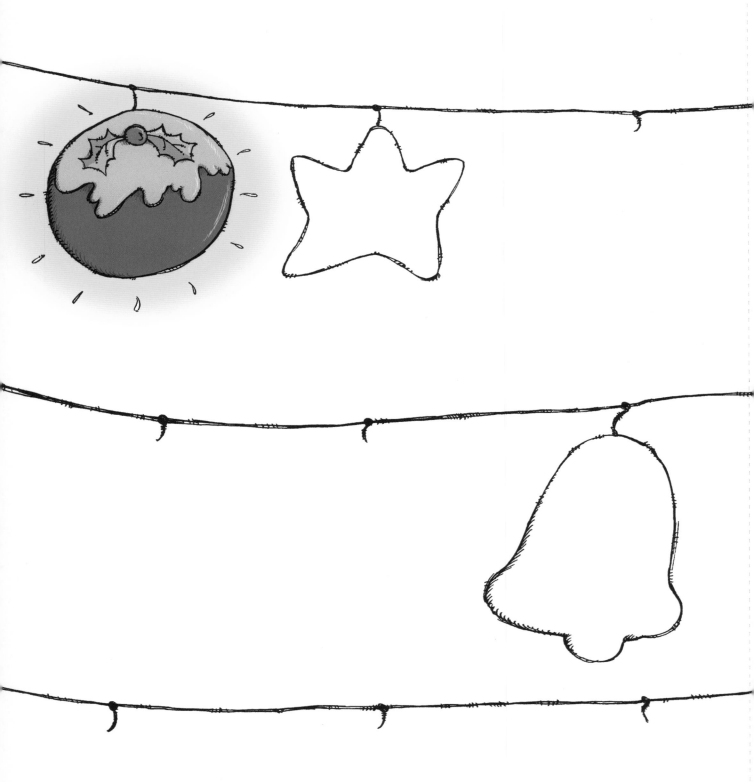

Draw Dad some wicked boots.

Help Santa get to the fireplace.

Put berries on the holly.

Fill the sky with robins.

Snowflakes glisten . . .

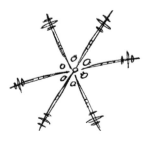

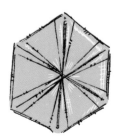

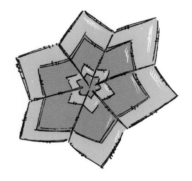

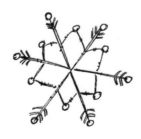

Put icicles around the window.

Build more snow animals.

Cookies or birds?

Snowball fight!

Give Dad the longest scarf ever.

Pop on some woolly hats.

What was outside on Christmas Eve?

Fill the basket with festive goodies.

What did Santa drop?

What is for Christmas dinner?

Who is singing carols?

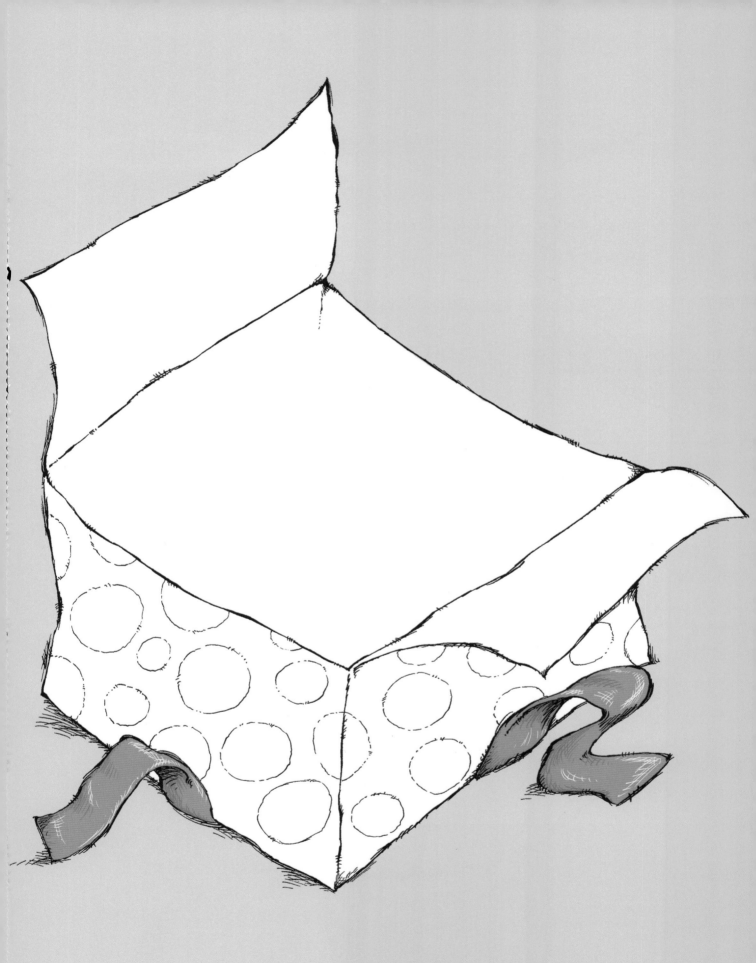

What is in the gift box?

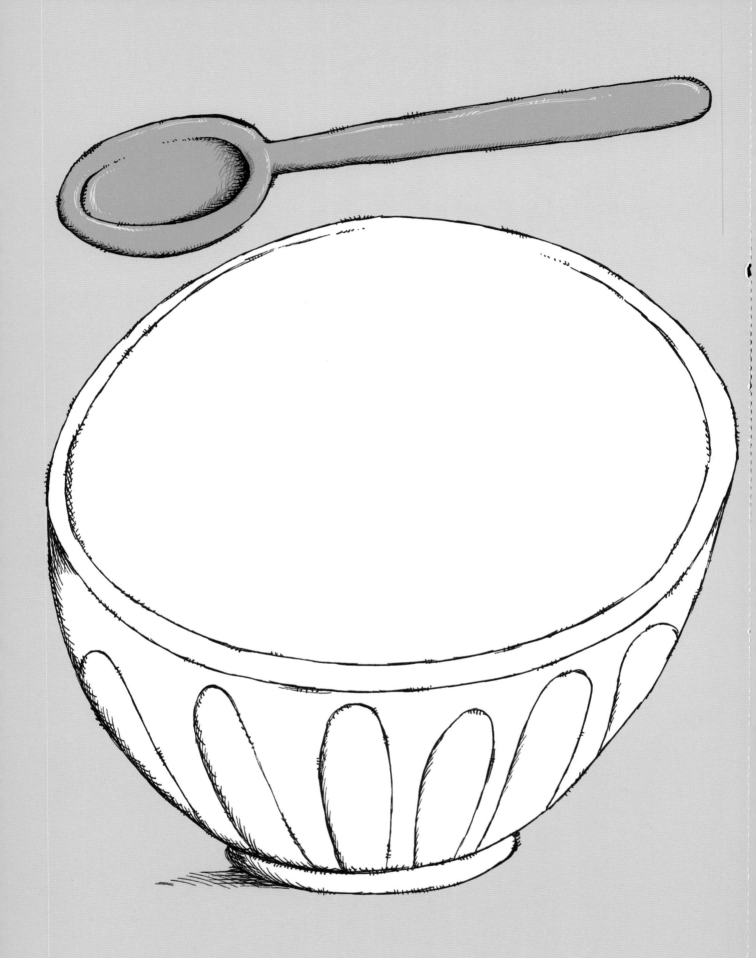

What is for dessert?

Who fell asleep after Christmas lunch?

Who ate the food?

What's in the sack?

Who made the snow angels?

Draw the Christmas parade.

Who is sledding?

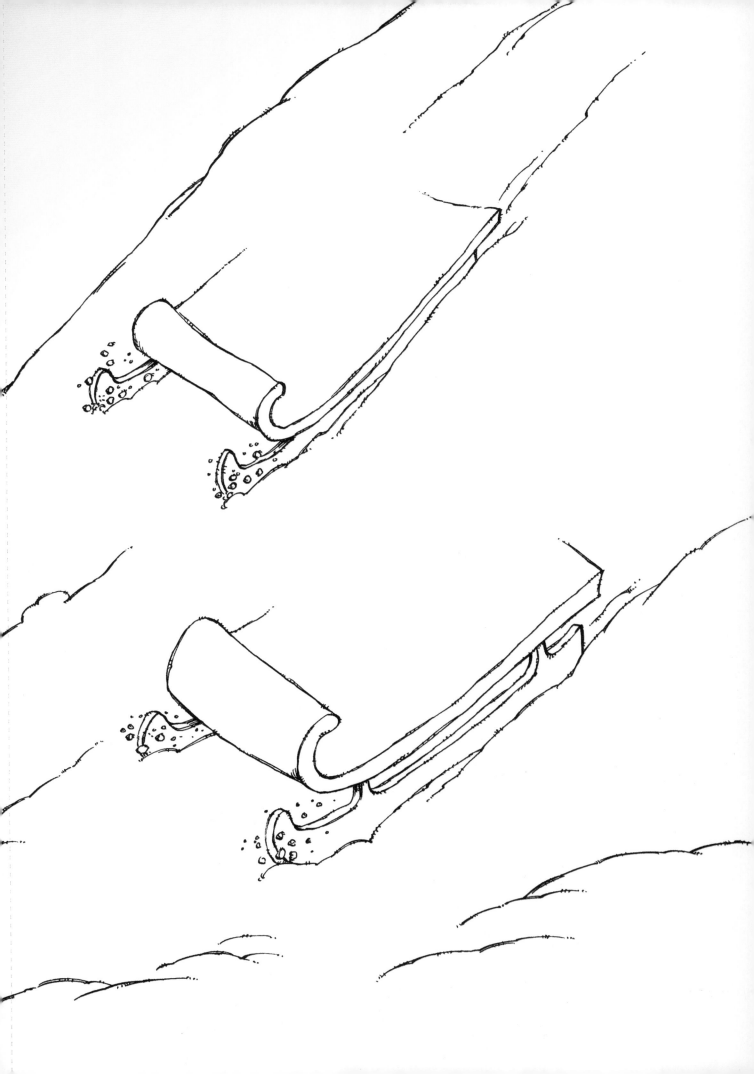

Put party hats on the puppies.

What is on next year's Christmas list?

The best present in the world.

The worst present in the world.

What is missing?

Which Christmas gifts will be regifted?

Decorate the angel's wings.

Oh, no! What has the turkey been stuffed with accidentally?

Complete the cute baby reindeer and give them names.

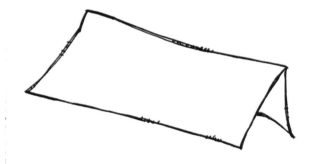

Finish the Christmas ornament.

Fill the box with festive treats.

Add some feathered friends and give them a tasty Christmas treat.

Complete the Christmas castle.

Add some flames for a
candlelit Christmas.

Decorate the dog's house.

Who's stuck in the giant snowball?

Decorate Santa's cozy quilt.

Holly or mistletoe?

Who's playing in the snow at the North Pole?

Complete Santa's house.

Give the astronaut a gift
that is out of this world.

What is in Santa's cave?

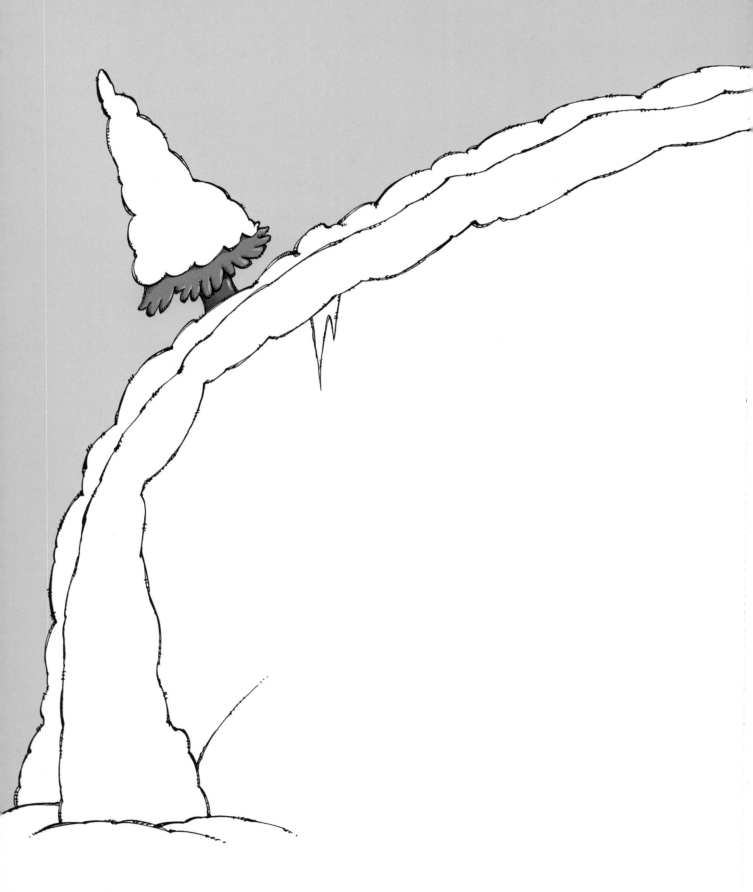

Fill the shoppers' bags
and boxes with gifts.

Make the sleigh look super for Santa.

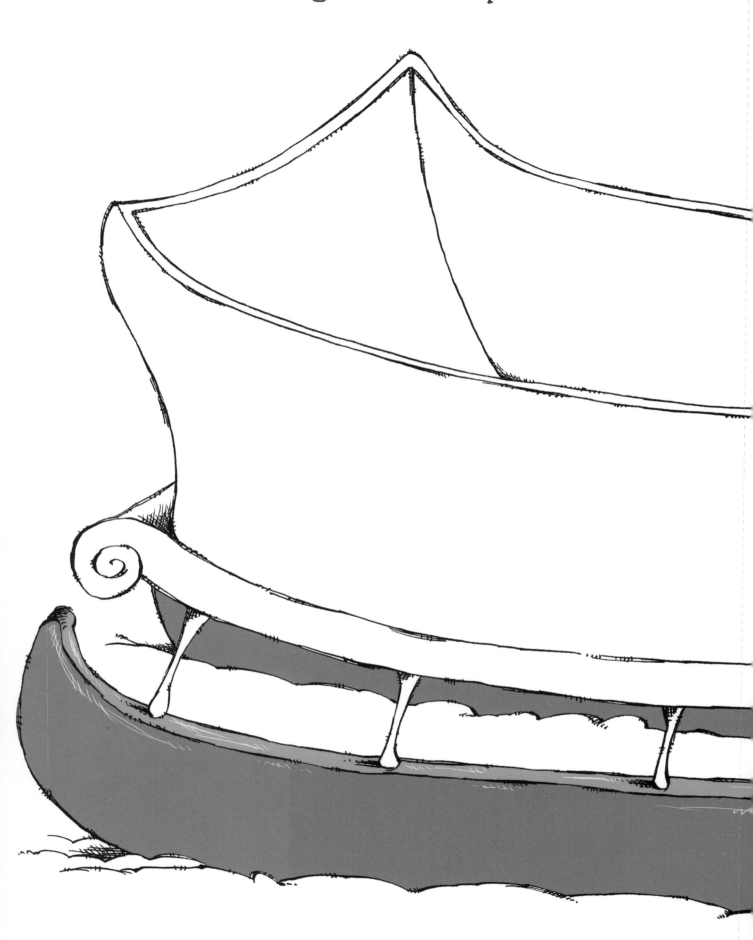

Fill it with gifts.

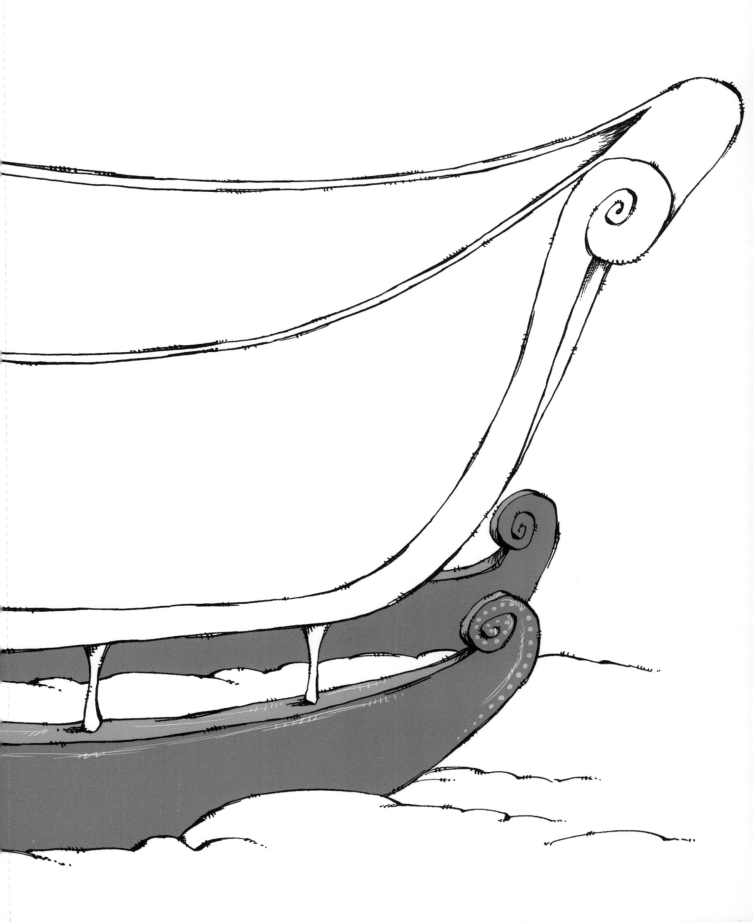

Who is waiting to see Santa?

Christmas trees or angels?

Cover the village in Christmas lights.

Make your New Year's resolutions.